THE BOOK OF

FECKIN'
IRISH
TRIVIA

THE BOOK OF FECKIN' IRISH TRIVIA

**Murphy & O'Dea's
Feckin' Collection**

THE O'BRIEN PRESS
DUBLIN

First published 2009 by The O'Brien Press Ltd
12 Terenure Road East, Rathgar, Dublin 6, Ireland.
Tel: +353 1 4923333; Fax: +353 1 4922777
E-mail: books@obrien.ie
Website: www.obrien.ie
Reprinted 2011.

ISBN: 978-1-84717-191-7

A catalogue record for this title is available from the British Library

2 3 4 5 6 7 8 9 10
11 12 13 14

Cover design: Colin Murphy/Donal O'Dea
Printed and bound by CPI Group (UK) Ltd, Croydon, CR0 4YY
The paper used in this book is produced using pulp from
managed forests

THANK YOU TO THESE TRULY TRIVIAL PEOPLE.

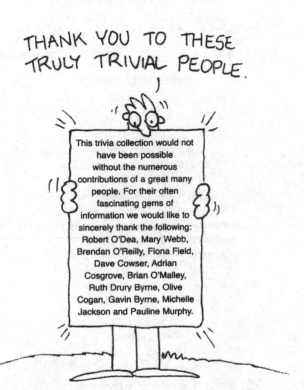

This trivia collection would not have been possible without the numerous contributions of a great many people. For their often fascinating gems of information we would like to sincerely thank the following: Robert O'Dea, Mary Webb, Brendan O'Reilly, Fiona Field, Dave Cowser, Adrian Cosgrove, Brian O'Malley, Ruth Drury Byrne, Olive Cogan, Gavin Byrne, Michelle Jackson and Pauline Murphy.

Muckanaghederdauhaulia
(22 letters), in County Galway is the
LONGEST PLACENAME in Ireland. It
is a townland and port and is the longest port
name in the world.

Although NUDISM is illegal
in Ireland, a recent survey listed Hawk
Cliff, Dalkey, Co. Dublin and Inch Beach,
Dingle, Co. Kerry as two of the top ten best
beaches in the world to let it all hang out.

Two of Britain's most
INFAMOUS MURDERERS, Burke & Hare,
who used to smother the elderly residents of
their lodging house in Edinburgh and sell
the bodies for medical research, were Irish.
When Burke was hanged, his body was
donated to the medical school. A pocket
book made of his skin is on display at the
Police Museum on the Royal Mile in
Edinburgh.

FORTY MILLION AMERICANS CLAIM IRISH LINEAGE.

An ancient Irish marriage ritual called
'handfasting', involved tying a rope between
the newlyweds' wrists for 366 days. It is said
that this is where the expression 'TYING
THE KNOT' originated.

Montgomery Street in Dublin was once the largest RED LIGHT DISTRICT in all of Europe, with over 1600 prostitutes plying their trade. A song called 'Take Me Up To Monto' sung by the Dubliners memorializes this area.

THE AVERAGE ANNUAL RAINFALL IN IRELAND IS ABOUT 150 CM.

The SMALLEST ever Irishman was David Jones from Lisburn in Antrim, who stood at 2 feet 2 inches when he died in 1970, aged 67.

THIN LIZZY took their name from a *Dandy* comic book robot character called 'Tin Lizzie'.

THERE ARE TWELVE TOWNS OR CITIES IN THE US CALLED DUBLIN.

WILLIAM HILL, one of Britain's biggest and well known bookmakers, was a Black & Tan in Ireland in 1919, stationed in Mallow, Co. Cork.

TWO TO ONE THIS ONE ENDS IN A DRAW.

Monserrat is the only other state that celebrates ST PATRICK'S DAY, as most of its population's ancestors were Irish slaves sent there by the English.

IRELAND'S SAINT FIACRE, BORN IN THE SIXTH CENTURY, IS THE PATRON SAINT OF GARDENERS.

The original Irish Houses of Parliament (which sat in what is now the Bank of Ireland, College Green, Dublin), was the WORLD'S FIRST purpose-built two-chamber parliament house.

Many historians believe that the game of rugby was invented, not as is commonly believed, when William Webb Ellis picked up the ball and ran at RUGBY School in England, but that his father, an officer, had been based in Ireland where he witnessed the game of 'Caid' being played – which involved much physical contact, running with a ball and trying to get it across a boundary, and that his son was simply demonstrating this sport. So the Irish, not the English, invented rugby!

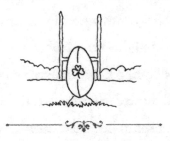

HITLER'S SISTER-IN-LAW WAS AN IRISH WOMAN CALLED BRIDGET DOWLING.

In 1952, one member of the
CENSORSHIP BOARD reviewed
seventy books in a three-month period and
banned all seventy.

**THE IRISH ALPHABET DOES
NOT CONTAIN THE LETTERS
J,K,Q,V,W,X,Y OR Z.**

Ballygally Castle in County Antrim,
nowadays a hotel, is said to be one of the
most haunted places in Ireland, thanks to
Lady Isobel Shaw, who supposedly knocks
on doors at night. Lady Isobel was reputedly
locked in her room and starved by her
husband during the 17th century, until she
finally leapt to her death from a window.

NIGHT NIGHT.
— SWEET DREAMS!

The cliffs at Croaghaun, Achill Island, at 668 metres, are said to be the HIGHEST SEA CLIFFS in Europe.

The 70's Celtic Rock Band 'HORSLIPS' took their name from a spoonerism on 'The Four Horsemen of the Apocalypse' which became 'The Four Poxmen on The Horslypse', eventually shortened to 'Horslips'.

CLARE IS KNOWN AS 'THE BANNER COUNTY' BECAUSE OF ITS FORMER TRADITION OF CARRYING BANNERS TO POLITICAL MEETINGS.

Ireland's most FAMOUS WITCH was Dame Alice Kyteler, born in Kilkenny in 1280. All four of her husbands died, and she was accused of poisoning them. In 1325, on the night before she was to be burned at the stake, she escaped and is believed to have fled to England. Her maid and follower, Petronilla de Meath, was burned instead. She was the first person in Ireland to be burned at the stake for witchcraft.

HERE LIES
PETRONILLA DE MEATH
THE UNLUCKIEST
MAID IN
IRELAND

The geographical centre of Ireland
is at a point in ROSCOMMON, 3km
south of Athlone.

**SAINT BRENDAN IS SAID TO HAVE
DISCOVERED AMERICA A THOUSAND
YEARS BEFORE COLUMBUS.**

COOOL! IS THIS PLACE LIKE, AWESOME OR WHAT?

The infamous Nazi
propaganda broadcaster, William Joyce,
aka LORD HAW HAW, was raised and
educated in Galway.

The Europa Hotel in Belfast is the
world's most BOMBED HOTEL,
having been blasted 33 times.

OVER 40% OF THE PRESIDENTS OF THE UNITED STATES HAD IRISH ANCESTORS.

Foxrock, Co. Dublin, is said to be the only village in Ireland WITHOUT A PUB.

In 1944 the CATHOLIC HIERARCHY asked the Minister for Public Health to ban tampons as they might 'stimulate young girls at an impressionable age', and the Government happily complied.

MORE THAN 150,000 IRISH MEN FOUGHT IN THE AMERICAN CIVIL WAR.

Irish physicist John Tyndall (1820-1893)
was the first person to explain why the
SKY IS BLUE.

SEE, IT'S STOPPED
RAINING. THAT'S WHY
THE SKY IS BLUE.

The lowest ever AIR TEMPERATURE
recorded in Ireland was -19.1°C at Markree
Castle, Co. Sligo on 16 January 1881.

MARKREE CASTLE

The phrase 'BY HOOK OR BY CROOK'
is said to have been coined by Richard de
Clare, aka Strongbow during the Norman
invasion of Ireland when he stated that he
would take Waterford by landing his army
at either Hook Head or by Crook village.

According to Teagasc, the Irish Agriculture and Food Development Authority, almost 10% of Ireland's entire BARLEY CROP is used in the making of Guinness.

IRISH-AMERICAN ARCHITECT LOUIS HENRI SULLIVAN IS CREDITED WITH THE INVENTION OF THE MODERN SKYSCRAPER.

Between the 1930s and 1950s, the Government employed hundreds of people to physically cut LINGERIE ADS out of foreign magazines, as they were considered to be of a sexually arousing nature.

During the Easter 1916 Rising, food for the big cats in DUBLIN ZOO was in such short supply that they killed some of the other animals to feed them.

In the 1934 Ireland v Belgium World Cup qualifier, which ended 4 - 4, Paddy Moore of SHAMROCK ROVERS became the first player in the world to score four goals in a World Cup game.

KEEP ON HOOPIN' PADDY.

Up to the late 1960s, women who had given birth were supposed to attend a ceremony called 'CHURCHING' which involved them being blessed and 'made pure again'.

The largest METEORITE ever
recorded in Ireland or Britain was part of a
shower that fell in Limerick on
10 September 1813. It weighed 48kg.

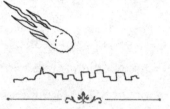

Astronomer Agnes Mary Clerke (1842-1907)
from Skibbereen is the only Irish person to
have a LUNAR CRATER named after her.

**261 PEOPLE IN IRELAND HAVE
HAD A HEART TRANSPLANT.**

The word 'STEEPLECHASE' originated
in 1752 from a cross-country horse race
between the steeples of Buttevant Church to
St. Leger Church in Doneraile, Co. Cork.

Before the ban on CONTRACEPTION was lifted in Ireland in the mid-1980s, it was fairly common practice to use clingfilm as a substitute for condoms.

DUBLIN'S LAST WORKHOUSE, IN SMITHFIELD, ONLY CLOSED DOWN IN 1969.

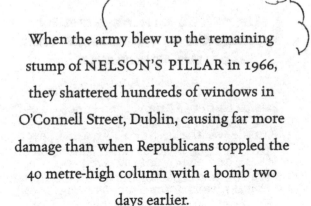

When the army blew up the remaining stump of NELSON'S PILLAR in 1966, they shattered hundreds of windows in O'Connell Street, Dublin, causing far more damage than when Republicans toppled the 40 metre-high column with a bomb two days earlier.

While filming RYAN'S DAUGHTER
in 1970/71, David Lean famously waited
for one year so he could shoot in a
storm of sufficient ferocity.

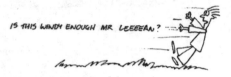

IS THIS WINDY ENOUGH MR LEEEEAN?

**UP TO 1892 THERE WERE 21
PLAYERS ON A GAA TEAM, 6 MORE
THAN AT PRESENT.**

Patrick Cotter O'Brien (1760 - 1806), from
Kinsale was the TALLEST Irishman ever
(8' 1") and one of only twelve people in
medical history to measure over eight feet.

The two species of RAT in Ireland
are the black and the brown, but the black
rat is exclusive to the tiny Lambay Island
off the coast of Dublin.

HEY! WHAT
ABOUT OUR
NEAR RELATIVES
UP IN LEINSTER
HOUSE?

**IN ANCIENT CELTIC IRELAND YOU
COULD DIVORCE YOUR PARTNER
BECAUSE HE/SHE WAS TOO FAT.**

THOMAS BRACKEN from
Monaghan, who became a successful
poet in New Zealand in the late 19th
century, wrote New Zealand's
National Anthem.

During an episode of
The 'LATE LATE SHOW' in the Sixties,
Gay Byrne held a mock version of 'Mr & Mrs',
during which he asked a contestant what she
wore on her honeymoon night. When she
replied 'nothing' there was a torrent of
complaints and condemnation.

**GIRLIE MAGAZINES LIKE
PLAYBOY WERE BANNED IN
IRELAND UNTIL 1996.**

During the first half of the nineteenth
century, the average number of CHILDREN
per household in Ireland was ten.

TO HAVE AND TO HOLD,
AND TO BREED LIKE RABBITS...

The biggest robbery in the history of the Irish Republic was on 26 February 2009, when 7 million Euro was stolen from the Bank of Ireland on College Green, Dublin.

IN 1991, DANIEL O'DONNELL OCCUPIED 6 OF THE TOP 7 PLACES IN THE UK COUNTRY MUSIC CHARTS.

In 1916 rebels seized the Dublin Wireless School of Telegraphy and began sending a message in Morse code, continuing for several days: 'Irish Republic declared in Dublin today. Irish troops have captured city and are in full possession. Enemy cannot move in city. The whole country rising.' This is generally accepted as the WORLD'S FIRST RADIO BROADCAST.

Ireland is the only country in the world
to have a musical instrument, THE HARP,
as its national symbol.

THERE ARE 4 COWS FOR EVERY PERSON IN LAOIS.

In 2002 a couple were arrested by
the Gardaí having been caught having
sex in the centre of CROKE PARK in
the middle of the night.

I'VE ALWAYS WANTED TO SCORE IN CROKER.

The word 'DONNYBROOK', meaning
a large fracas, originated from Donnybrook
Fair, the annual scene of much drunken
brawling, so much, in fact, that the fair
was banned in 1855.

The first floodlit GAA game in Croke Park
in 2007 between Dublin and Tyrone was
disrupted by Croke Park's first ever
STREAKER, a nineteen-year-old man.

UP THE DUBS!

MUHAMMAD ALI'S GREAT GRANDFATHER WAS IRISH. ABE GRADY WAS BORN IN ENNIS IN 1842.

The capstone of the Brownshill Dolmen
in County Carlow weighs approximately
100 metric tons and is the heaviest such
megalithic stone in Europe.

The largest island off Ireland's coast
is Achill at 145 square km.

**IN PRE-CHRISTIAN
IRELAND POLYGAMY WAS
WIDELY PRACTISED.**

The fight between John Wayne
and Victor McLaglen in 'The Quiet
Man' is the LONGEST BRAWL in
cinema history.

The remains of ST VALENTINE, the patron
saint of love, whose feast day is celebrated
on 14 February, are buried in Dublin's
Whitefriar Street church.

BUCK WHALEY was the notorious gambling, hard-drinking, whoring son of a wealthy landowner in the late eighteenth century, who, at the age of 16, lost £14,000 in a single night in a Paris casino (millions in today's money). He would accept virtually any bet, and when challenged to live on Irish soil while residing outside the country, he duly imported tons of Irish soil to the Isle of Man and built a house on it.

HURLING IS THE WORLD'S FASTEST FIELD TEAM SPORT.

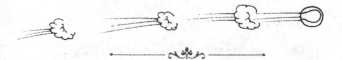

German pilots believed they were over a British city when they DROPPED BOMBS on Dublin in 1941. Thirty-eight people died.

Nuns used to ban girls from wearing
SHINY SHOES in the Fifties and Sixties
in case boys could see a reflection in them
of the girls' knickers.

**AT ONE POINT, PRE-GAELIC
ATHLETIC ASSOCIATION, SLIOTARS
(HURLING BALLS) WERE
MADE OF HOLLOW BRONZE.**

Viagra, the famous drug that's been giving
people's sex lives a lift the world over, was
mass-produced for the first time in
Ringaskiddy, Co. Cork.

The world-famous BOOK OF KELLS
was made from the skin of about 200 cows
and the ink from a mixture of apple
juice and soot.

In 1845, William Parsons built a 72-inch REFLECTING TELESCOPE near Birr in Offaly which remained the largest telescope in the world for 70 years.

FUNGI THE DOLPHIN HAS BEEN RESIDENT IN DINGLE BAY FOR OVER A QUARTER OF A CENTURY.

Up to the thirteenth century in Ireland it was commonplace for PRIESTS and MONKS to have wives, girlfriends and children.

FATHER, CAN I HAVE MY POCKETMONEY?

The TALLEST STRUCTURE in the Republic of Ireland is the transmitter near Tullamore, Co. Offaly which stands at 290m.

Jackie Carey of Manchester United
captained Ireland when they beat
England 2-0 in Goodison Park in 1949,
becoming the first team to DEFEAT
ENGLAND AT HOME. Carey played
in nine different positions in his career,
including goalkeeper.

**DUBLIN'S O'CONNELL BRIDGE IS
WIDER THAN IT IS LONG.**

250 million years ago, Ireland was at the
same LATITUDE as present day Egypt.

The name of the British political party, the TORIES, originates from an old Gaelic word '*toraidhe*', meaning plunderer.

DUBLIN HAS 1147.3 PEOPLE PER SQUARE KILOMETRE.

LOUGH REE, situated on the Shannon, between Longford and Westmeath, is said to be home to a 'Loch Ness' type monster.

Well-known Irish movie actor COLIN FARRELL auditioned to become a member of the successful boyband Boyzone, but was rejected.

The highest ever ATTENDANCE at a sporting event in Ireland was 90,556, at the 1961 All-Ireland Senior Football Final between Offaly and Down.

THE SUN SETS IN GALWAY ALMOST ONE FULL HOUR AFTER IT HAS SET IN LONDON.

In 1940/41 HITLER'S propaganda minister, Goebbels, commissioned two anti-British, pro-Irish rebel movies called 'The Fox of Glenarvon' and 'My Life for Ireland', with German actors playing all the Irish roles.

VALENTIA ISLAND IN KERRY IS THE MOST WESTERLY POINT IN EUROPE THAT IS INHABITED.

Because HENRY MOORE, Earl of Drogheda owned land in Dublin, he decided to name a street or two after himself as the land was developed. Thus we got Henry Street, Moore Street, North Earl Street and Drogheda Street, which is now O'Connell Street.

THE TITANIC COST $7.5 MILLION TO BUILD. THE MOVIE 'TITANIC' COST $200 MILLION.

The SMALLEST IRISHWOMAN on record was Catherine Kelly who died in England in 1785 and was just 2' 10" tall.

A survey on Tripadvisor.com voted the
BLARNEY STONE the most unhygienic
tourist attraction in the world.

**IRELAND HAS THE HIGHEST BIRTH RATE
IN THE EU.**

The same survey voted
OSCAR WILDE'S TOMB in Père
Lachaise Cemetery, Paris, as the third
most unhygienic tourist attraction -
it is covered in lipstick prints!

Maumtrasna Mountain on the
Galway-Mayo border covers a total surface
area of almost 40 square kilometres.

When RED HUGH O'DONNELL
escaped from Dublin Castle in 1592, along with
Art and Henry O'Neill, they became the only
prisoners ever to successfully escape captivity in
Dublin Castle.

I KNEW I SHOULDN'T HAVE LEFT MY
BOLT CUTTERS LYING AROUND.

The phrase 'HE DIGS WITH
HIS RIGHT/LEFT FOOT' denoting
one's religion, originated in Ulster,
where Catholics generally used a spade
with a lug on the left and Protestants with one
on the right.

The lion that originally appeared
in the METRO-GOLDWYN-MAYER
logo was called 'Slats' and was born
in Dublin Zoo in 1919.

**THE CONOR PASS IN KERRY IS THE
HIGHEST MOUNTAIN PASS IN IRELAND.**

MAGPIES and Cromwell first
arrived in Ireland around the same time
and both landed in Wexford. Because of
this, many people directly linked the birds with
the invaders and believed Ireland would never
be free of the English until we
were rid of the magpies.

DAMN
MAGPIES!

Ireland's OLDEST NEWSPAPER
is the *Belfast News Letter* which was
founded in 1737.

**IN THE 17TH CENTURY,
YOUGHAL COUNCIL, COUNTY CORK,
INTRODUCED A FINE OF £50 FOR
DEFLOWERING THE DAUGHTER
OF AN ALDERMAN.**

In the early 1900s, ALOIS HITLER,
half brother of Adolf Hitler, worked in the
Shelbourne Hotel, Dublin.

Dominic West, the actor who plays Detective JIMMY MCNULTY in 'The Wire', was educated at Trinity College, Dublin.

ROSSLARE IN WEXFORD IS THE SUNNIEST TOWN IN IRELAND, WITH 4.3 HOURS OF SUNSHINE PER DAY.

ST OLIVER PLUNKETT'S head is on display in St Peter's Church in Drogheda, Co Louth. Some of the rest of his body is in Bath in England and the remainder is in Germany.

THE LIFE EXPECTANCY FOR A WOMAN IN IRELAND IS 80.88 YEARS.

Since 2004, 150,000 POLISH PEOPLE
have immigrated to Ireland and there are
now more Polish speakers than Irish
speakers in the country.

FINGALIAN was a language of Old
English and Nordic origins that was
spoken in the Fingal area of Dublin
until the 1800s.

In the seventeenth century
ST STEPHEN'S GREEN, Dublin was a
piece of marsh surrounded by a wall.

According to international death rates (per thousand per annum), an Irish person is FOUR TIMES more likely to die in a given year than someone from the United Arab Emirates.

ICELAND WAS FIRST SETTLED BY A GROUP OF IRISH MONKS KNOWN AS 'THE PAPAR'.

The 1968/69 season of RTÉ's 'The Late Late Show' was presented by FRANK HALL, as Gay Byrne was working with the BBC.

TO WHOM IT MAY CONCERN...
GAY BYRNE HAS LEFT THE BUILDING

'BILLY THE BOWL' was a legless murderer who got around Dublin in a tin bowl in the late 18th century. He turned from begging to robbery and murder and was eventually hanged in 1786.

When ALI fought Al Lewis in Croke Park in 1972, he was so desperate for a pee at the end of the tenth round that he launched a sustained attack on his opponent and finished him off in the 11th.

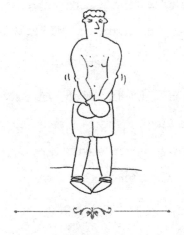

In 1973 the IRA landed a helicopter in the
exercise yard of Mountjoy Prison and
rescued their Chief-of-staff Joe Tierney.

There are 120 recognised saints
buried in the church graveyard of St Eanna
on the Aran Island of INISHMORE.

JACK KELLY, father of Irish-American
actress and later Princess, Grace Kelly, was the
first person ever to win three Olympic
Gold medals for rowing.

The Church of Ireland BISHOP OF RAPHOE, Philip Twysden, was shot dead while carrying out a robbery on a stagecoach in London in 1752.

BEATLE GEORGE HARRISON'S GRANDFATHER, JOHN FRENCH, WAS BORN IN WEXFORD.

Until recently, there was a law on Ireland's statute books making it illegal to enhance PROFITS ON COFFEE SALES by mixing it with sheep dung.

Ireland has more mobile phones per capita
than any other country in Europe.

THERE ARE 46 RIVERS IN DUBLIN.

Bram Stoker, the Irish author
of *Dracula*, never visited eastern Europe
in his entire lifetime.

**THE BOG OF ALLEN IS ALMOST
1000 SQUARE KILOMETRES IN SIZE.**

When MARY McALEESE replaced
Mary Robinson as Irish President, it became
the first time in the world that one female
president had succeeded another.

In the 17th century, the British paid a
£20 BOUNTY for every priest caught by
a bounty hunter.

The highest ever TEMPERATURE
recorded in Ireland was 33.3°C at Kilkenny
Castle on 26 June 1887.

The WESTLINK BRIDGE across Dublin's
River Liffey, which handles 21,000 vehicles a
day, is the busiest bridge in Europe.

Croghan-Kinsella was the site of Ireland's only GOLD RUSH, in 1795, when a nugget was found in river gravel on the mountain. Three thousand ounces of gold were found before the gold was exhausted.

ASTRONAUT NEIL ARMSTRONG'S ANCESTORS WERE FROM FERMANAGH.

Ceide Fields in Mayo was the site of the largest known STONE AGE COMMUNITY in Europe, with as many as 5,000 inhabitants at its peak.

Dublin's North BULL WALL was designed by Captain William Bligh, he of the infamous Mutiny on the Bounty.

IN IRISH LAW, 14,500 ACTS PRE-DATE THE ACT OF UNION OF 1801.

One of the few survivors of the famous Russian uprising or mutiny on the Battleship Potemkin in 1905, was IVAN BESHOFF, who made it to Dublin and opened the city's famous Beshoff fish and chip shop, which is still in operation today.

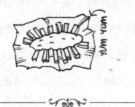

The SMALLEST CHURCH in
Ireland is St Gobhans at Portbradden in
Antrim, measuring just 10' x 6'.

CONEY ISLAND in New York was
named after a tiny island off Sligo by an
Irish captain, Peter O'Connor, in the
eighteenth century.

**THE ROTUNDA IN DUBLIN,
OPENED IN 1745, WAS THE WORLD'S
FIRST PURPOSE-BUILT MATERNITY
HOSPITAL.**

The UNION JACK contains
a red saltire or diagonal cross called
St Patrick's Cross, representing Ireland.
There is no cross for Wales.

Up to the 1920s, couples in Teltown, Co. Meath could get MARRIED simply by walking towards each other.

LEITRIM IS IRELAND'S LEAST POPULOUS COUNTY WITH JUST 15.7 INHABITANTS PER SQUARE KILOMETRE.

CAHIRCIVEEN CATHOLIC CHURCH, Co. Kerry is the only one in Ireland named after a layman - Daniel O'Connell.

Ireland is more DENSELY POPULATED than the United States of America and Russia.

At the peak of Fr Theobald Mathew's Temperance Movement around 1850, over three million Irish people had taken 'THE PLEDGE' i.e. not to drink alcohol again.

CEMENT WAS INVENTED IN 1789 BY BRYAN HIGGINS FROM SLIGO.

Cornelscourt, Co. Dublin, was Ireland's first SHOPPING CENTRE. It opened in 1966.

THERE ARE OVER 40,000 BASALT COLUMNS IN THE GIANT'S CAUSEWAY IN COUNTY ANTRIM.

The first PANTOMIME in Ireland, 'The Magic Rose', was staged at the Theatre Royal in Dublin in 1811.

The first action of the Easter 1916 RISING took place in Laois, not Dublin, when Volunteers blew up a section of railway track on 23 April, one day before a shot was fired in the capital.

IRISH WRITERS HAVE BEEN AWARDED THE NOBEL PRIZE FOR LITERATURE FOUR TIMES – YEATS, SHAW, BECKETT AND HEANEY.

The HELL FIRE CLUB on Montpelier Hill, south Dublin, was originally the scene of orgies of drinking, gambling and wanton sex among wealthy young individuals of the late 1700s. The motto of this group was 'Do as you will.'

The Old MILITARY ROAD in Wicklow was built by the British to help fight Michael Dwyer, who had been successfully fighting a guerilla war against them in the hills for over six years after the 1798 rebellion.

THE ANTLERS OF THE NOW EXTINCT IRISH ELK COULD MEASURE AS MUCH AS TWELVE FEET ACROSS.

Although Irish, the DUKE OF WELLINGTON, who defeated Napoleon at Waterloo, was not proud of his roots and is reputed to have said: 'being born in a stable does not make one a horse.'

COUNTY CORK IS NINE TIMES THE SIZE OF COUNTY LOUTH.

THOMAS MOORE'S statue in College Green, Dublin shares a traffic island with a public toilet. The statue's nickname is 'The meeting of the waters', thus honouring his famous poem and the nearby public convenience.

A KELPIE is a supernatural water horse, believed to haunt the lakes of Ireland, which can transform itself into a handsome man to lure women into the water, drown them and eat them.

I'M HAVING SOME FRIENDS OVER FOR DINNER...

Ireland was hit by its worst ever STORM in 1839 when wind speed reached over 125 mph, killing hundreds of people.

The earliest reference to Dublin is
in the writings of the GREEK cartographer
Ptolemy in AD140, who called the
settlement 'Eblana'.

The sub-atomic term 'ELECTRON'
was introduced by Irish physicist George
Johnstone Stoney in 1891.

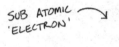

SUB ATOMIC
'ELECTRON'

**IF YOU HEAR A BANSHEE'S
WAIL, SOMEONE'S ABOUT TO
KICK THE BUCKET.**

In Irish mythology, ACHTLAND
was a mortal woman who could not find a
human male to satisfy her sexual needs
so took a giant from the race of Tuatha Dé
Danann as her mate.

When Irish scientist Mary Ward
was killed by a steam-powered automobile
driven by her cousin in 1869, she officially
became the world's first ROAD
TRAFFIC ACCIDENT victim.

MAKE SURE... THAT... THEY... KNOW...
I WAS... THE FIRST!

**IRELAND IS THE TWENTIETH-
LARGEST ISLAND IN THE WORLD.
GREENLAND IS No. 1.**

The first European to set foot on American
soil was not Christopher Columbus but
Irishman PATRICK MAGUIRE, who was
a member of the crew.

Irish-American actor AUDIE MURPHY, who was a top Hollywood star of the Fifties, was the most decorated soldier of WWII, receiving 28 citations for bravery, including the Medal of Honor.

The first POTATOES in Europe were grown by Sir Walter Raleigh in 1596 on his estate in Youghal, County Cork.

THERE ARE 628 KNOWN MEGALITHIC TOMBS IN IRELAND.

The man who designed the O'Connell Monument in Dublin, JOHN HENRY FOLEY, also designed the Albert Memorial in London.

While playing for Manchester City against Derby County in 1991, NIALL QUINN scored for his team, then took over in goal when City's keeper was sent off. He then saved a penalty and City won the game 2 – 1.

YOU AIN'T SEEN NOTHING LIKE THE MIGHTY QUINN

The PASSWORD for George Washington's troops in Boston in 1776, the year of US Independence, was 'St Patrick'.

Dublin's first BUS ROUTE was started
by the Clondalkin Omnibus Company
in 1919. The vehicle was a horse-drawn
wooden structure resting on a 5 ton chassis.

BET IT STILL GOT
IN TO TOWN QUICKER.

BUS

THE IRISH WOLFHOUND IS THE TALLEST DOG BREED IN THE WORLD.

In 1795, a Belfast doctor and poet, William
Drennar, was the first to coin the phrase:
'THE EMERALD ISLE'.

LOUGH DERG (meaning red lake) in Donegal gets its name from the legend of St Patrick killing a serpent in the lake, the blood turning the water red.

Takabuti, the first MUMMY to be seen publicly outside of Egypt, was displayed in Belfast in 1831 and is still on display at the Ulster Museum.

The Irish theologian and philosopher JOHANNES SCOTUS ERIUGENA (815–877) was once asked by King Charles the Bald of France 'What separates a drunkard from an Irishman?' to which Johannes replied, 'Only a table'.

I MAY BE DRUNK BUT AT LEAST I'M NOT A BALDY FECKER LIKE YOU

Famous Irish writer and wit OSCAR WILDE'S full name was Oscar Fingal O'Flahertie Wills Wilde.

ARTHUR GUINNESS HAD 21 CHILDREN.

During the famine in 1847, the CHOCTAW INDIANS from south east USA raised $710 for famine relief, the equivalent today of about one million dollars.

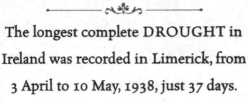

The longest complete DROUGHT in Ireland was recorded in Limerick, from 3 April to 10 May, 1938, just 37 days.

CORK GETS ITS NAME FROM THE IRISH WORD *CORCACH* MEANING 'MARSH'.

There are actually two O'CONNELL BRIDGES in Dublin. One spans the Liffey and the other crosses the pond in St Stephen's Green.

A law originally on the Irish statute books made it illegal for a student to walk through TRINITY COLLEGE without wearing a sword.

Ireland's most northerly point is
INISHTRAHULL ISLAND, 7 km north
of the Donegal coast.

**IN 1840 ONLY HALF THE IRISH
POPULATION COULD READ OR WRITE.**

Trinity College LIBRARY is legally
entitled to a copy of every book published
in Great Britain and Ireland. The library
currently has 4.5 million books.

HAND IT OVER

Being awarded the FREEDOM OF
DUBLIN gives you the right to graze sheep
on College Green.

Ireland has had four major
CURRENCY changes in 40 years – the
pound sterling (pounds, shillings and
pence) replaced by the decimal pound in
1971, replaced by the Irish pound in 1978,
replaced by the Euro in 2002.

A 'MERROW' is the Celtic
equivalent of a mermaid, said to reveal
their naked upper bodies to young men to
lure them into the sea.

THE WATER'S FREEZIN'?

The 1964 musical 'MY FAIR LADY'
was based on George Bernard Shaw's play
'Pygmalion'.

The Great STALACTITE in Doolin Cave, Co. Clare, is the world's largest free-hanging stalactite.

According to an ancient Irish superstition, having a haircut on GOOD FRIDAY will prevent you getting headaches for a year.

EDWARD BRUCE, brother of the more famous Robert, King of Scotland, was once crowned King of Ireland.

The Academy Award's 'OSCAR' statuette was designed by Cedric Gibbons, who was born in Dublin.

ONLY 20% OF IRISH PRIMARY SCHOOL TEACHERS ARE MALE.

Katherine Plunket, an aristocrat from Co. Louth, was the oldest Irish person ever. She died in 1932 aged 111.

ST. PATRICK'S NAME AT BIRTH WAS MAEWYN SUCCAT.

I CAN SEE WHY HE CHANGED IT.

Irish scientist John Joly from Offaly was the first man to use RADIATION to treat cancerous tumours.

There were about 120 Irish passengers on the TITANIC, most of whom died. One Irish girl, called Anna Kelly, who had gone on deck to find out what had happened, survived and later became a nun.

LEITRIM ONLY GOT ITS FIRST SET OF TRAFFIC LIGHTS IN 2003.

NOW ALL WE NEED IS SOME TRAFFIC!

The correct title for Irishman Jonathan Swift's famous novel *Gulliver's Travels* is *Travels into Several Remote Nations of the World, in Four Parts. By Lemuel Gulliver, First a Surgeon, and then a Captain of several Ships.*

The longest HUNGER STRIKE in world
history was by 9 republicans in Cork prison
in 1920. They went 94 days without food.

It was when over-flying Ireland in
a plane that JOHNNY CASH was inspired
to write the song 'Forty Shades of Green'.

**TORR HEAD IN ANTRIM IS JUST
23KM FROM SCOTLAND.**

The first ever ST PATRICK'S DAY
PARADE was held in New York on
17 March, 1762 by Irish soldiers who
were serving in the British Army.

According to *The Times History of the War*, both sides ceased fire briefly during the 1916 Rising to allow the St. Stephen's Green PARK KEEPER, Joseph Kearney, to feed the wide variety of waterfowl in the park.

IN HURLING, A SLIOTAR CAN TRAVEL AT SPEEDS OF UP TO 150 KPH.

In a 2002 BBC Global Service poll, 'A Nation Once Again' was voted the WORLD'S MOST POPULAR SONG.

Louis Brennan from Castlebar invented the STEERABLE TORPEDO and the world's first trials took place in Crosshaven, Cork.

The body that preceded the Irish Censorship Board was called 'The Committee on EVIL LITERATURE'.

Bushmills in Antrim is the oldest WHISKEY DISTILLERY in the world still in operation. It is 401 years old.

IRELAND'S FIRST CINEMA, THE VOLTA IN MARY STREET, DUBLIN, OPENED IN 1909.

Thirteen COUNTIES have yet to register an All Ireland Senior Football Championship win – Wicklow, Carlow, Monaghan, Longford, Westmeath, Laois, Kilkenny, Waterford, Clare, Sligo, Leitrim, Fermanagh and Antrim.

The last survivor of the 1789
MUTINY ON THE BOUNTY
was John Adams from Derry.

In the 1970s BOB GELDOF worked
in an abattoir, a pea canning factory and
as a road navvy.

**ALTHOUGH THE GAME OF POLO
ORIGINATED IN PERSIA, IT WAS
FIRST PLAYED IN EUROPE IN
LIMERICK IN 1868.**

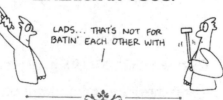

LADS... THAT'S NOT FOR
BATIN' EACH OTHER WITH

Between AD500-800 IRELAND'S
MONASTIC SETTLEMENTS had the
status in Europe in educational terms that
Harvard, Yale or Oxford enjoy today.

When JM Synge's play
'THE PLAYBOY OF THE WESTERN
WORLD' premiered in the Abbey Theatre,
Dublin in 1907, there were riots as the play was
believed to have 'cast a slight on the virtue
of Irish womanhood'.

LORD EDWARD FITZGERALD,
who was one of the leaders of the 1798
rebellion, was also an officially adopted
Chief of the Huron Tribe of North
American Indians.

Up until 1996, any visitor to the
Hideout Pub in Kilcullen, Kildare, could
view the arm that brought legendary Irish
world champion boxer Dan Donnelly such
success. After he died in 1820 his body was
stolen by graverobbers for medical research
and eventually a travelling salesman
purchased the SEVERED SKELETAL
ARM and sold it to the pub's owner who
put it on display in a glass case.

**IRELAND HAS MORE DOGS
PER CAPITA THAN ANY OTHER
COUNTRY IN EUROPE.**

NEWGRANGE passage tomb
was built 500 years before the
Great Pyramid at Giza.

The green, white and orange of the
IRISH TRICOLOUR was inspired by the
red, white and blue of the French tricolour
after Thomas Francis Meagher had visited
Paris during a period of revolution.

VIVA LES PADDIES

'Gentleman' JIM CORBETT, the famous
Irish-American boxer, reputedly soaked his
bandages in Plaster of Paris before a fight.

A statue of William of Orange that once
stood opposite Trinity College was blown up in
1946. It was the last EQUESTRIAN
STATUE in Dublin.

SHEELA NA GIGS are ancient
stone carvings of a female figure openly
displaying her genitals, often found on
church walls around Ireland. There are
over 100 in Ireland and they are thought
to have warded off evil spirits.

**BEATLE JOHN LENNON'S
GRANDFATHER, JACK LENNON,
AND GRANDMOTHER, MARY
MAGUIRE, WERE IRISH.**

Galway-born actor PETER O'TOOLE
has been nominated eight times for an
Oscar as Best Actor in a Leading Role, giving
him a unique record as the most nominated
actor never to have won the award.

**IN 2005, THERE WAS ONE PUB FOR
EVERY 350 PEOPLE IN IRELAND.**

The hypodermic SYRINGE was invented by Dubliner Dr Francis Rynd in 1845 and the first injection in the world was administered at the Meath Hospital.

PAUL McCARTNEY'S father and grandfather were born in Ireland and his grandfather's character was portrayed by Wilfrid Brambell in the movie 'A Hard Day's Night'.

Fishamble Street in Dublin's Temple Bar was
the location of the first performance of
HANDEL'S MESSIAH in April 1742.

**THE FIRST IRISH CONSTITUTION
WAS SIGNED IN ROOM 112 OF THE
SHELBOURNE HOTEL, DUBLIN, IN 1922.**

An Irishwoman, Jennie Hodgers from
Louth, served for the duration of the US
Civil War disguised AS A MAN.

GEORGE BEST Belfast City Airport
is the only airport in the world named
after a footballer.

If the Belfast-built ship 'TITANIC' had hit the iceberg head-on, in all probability it would have stayed afloat.

NOW HE TELLS US...

In 1920, during the War of Independence, British officer COL. SMYTH issued an order that if a man approached a barricade with his hands in his pockets he was to be shot.

IRELAND'S COASTLINE MEASURES 1,448 KILOMETRES.

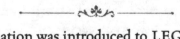

Legislation was introduced to LEGALISE CONDOMS in Ireland in 1979, making them available to over-18s on prescription. This was two years older than the legal age at which you could marry.

The Irish Proclamation was one
of the first such documents in the world
to recognize the EQUALITY of men
and women.

NO, YOU'RE NOT PAID LESS
BECAUSE YOU'RE A WOMAN!
WE'RE JUST PAID MORE
CAUSE WE'RE MEN.

**THE IRISH ARE THE BIGGEST
PER CAPITA CONSUMERS OF TEA
IN THE WORLD.**

In 2008 an ORANG-UTAN escaped its
enclosure and spent an hour wandering
around Dublin Zoo.

The only reptile species native to Ireland
is the VIVIPAROUS LIZARD, found
mainly in the south west.

**ST COLUMCILLE IS THE PATRON SAINT
OF BOOKBINDERS AND POETS.**

The windows in the Bank of Ireland,
College Green were bricked up to avoid
paying 'window tax'. It was this tax that
allegedly gave rise to the term
'DAYLIGHT ROBBERY'.

The *GUINNESS BOOK OF RECORDS*
came into existence because Sir Hugh Beaver,
MD of Guinness, got into an
argument while hunting in Wexford over
which was the fastest game bird in Europe,
the golden plover or the grouse.

YOLA is a now-extinct Germanic
language that was spoken in south Wexford
up to the mid-nineteenth century.

The WETTEST DAY ever recorded
somewhere in Ireland was at Cloore Lake
Co. Kerry on 18 September 1993, when
243.5mm of rain fell.

The HAROLD'S CROSS area in Dublin
is said to derive its name from the name of
a gallows which was erected in the 14th century
on the spot now occupied by Harold's Cross
Park. It continued to be a place of
execution until the 18th century.

THIS PLACE
IS DEADLY!

Although a pacifist, in 1815 DANIEL O'CONNELL shot and killed John D'Esterre, a member of Dublin Corporation, in a duel.

HMMM. SORRY ABOUT THAT.

2000 MEN WERE (LEGALLY) EXECUTED IN IRELAND IN THE 19TH CENTURY.

Adolf Hitler had a contingency plan to INVADE IRELAND codenamed 'Operation Emerald'.

CORK HARBOUR is the world's
second largest natural harbour after
Sydney Harbour.

**THERE ARE 64 TOWNS IN IRELAND
BEGINNING WITH THE PREFIX 'BALLY'.**

In 1968, a 1000-year-old block of
cheese was found PRESERVED in a
bog in Tipperary.

In the mid-17th century, Oliver
Cromwell ordered the burning of all
HARPS found in Ireland.

In 1995, a priest in Dungarvan announced
from the pulpit that a local woman had
deliberately slept with 60 men from the
town in order to infect them with AIDS.

**IN 2006, THERE WERE 2,494 MORE
WOMEN THAN MEN IN IRELAND.**

The coach used by The Queen at the State
Opening of Parliament is called
the IRISH STATE COACH because the
original was built in 1851 by the Lord
Mayor of Dublin, John Reynolds, who
was also a coachbuilder

**IN 1800, THE POPULATION
OF IRELAND WAS TWICE THAT
OF THE UNITED STATES.**

'THE PALE' was an area in the twelfth century that included Dublin, Meath, Louth and part of Kildare. Anyone from outside this was considered to be a bit of a savage, thus 'Beyond the pale.'

IRISH WOMEN GOT THE VOTE IN 1928.

Since its founding in 1968, KNOCK MARRIAGE BUREAU in County Mayo has been instrumental in bringing about almost 1000 marriages.

The last person to be publicly executed in the UK was Irishman MICHAEL BARRETT who was wrongly hanged for the Clerkenwell bombings of 1867.

Ronald Reagan hushed up his
IRISH ROOTS before he was elected
President because he was afraid it would
turn some voters against him.

According to Limerick-born actor Richard
Harris, the mansion he owned in England
was HAUNTED by an eight-year-old boy
who he could hear running around, banging
doors and generally keeping him awake. He
managed to placate the spirit somewhat by
having a nursery, complete with toys and
games, built in a tower of the mansion.

The Roman name for Ireland,
HIBERNIA, comes from the Latin
hibernus, which means 'wintry'.

**ENYA IS IRELAND'S MOST
SUCCESSFUL SOLO ARTIST, WITH
SALES OF OVER 70 MILLION ALBUMS.**

The giant sea-stack at DUN BRISTE,
Mayo was connected to the land by an arch
as recently as 1393. When it collapsed, the
people living there had to be rescued by
climbing across the newly-created chasm on
ships' ropes. No one returned to the top of
Dun Briste until the twentieth century.

There was once a town with nine named streets on the island of Bannow in Wexford, built in the 12th century. In the 17th century the channel separating the island from the mainland silted up and the shifting sands eventually completely buried the town, which became known for a time as the IRISH HERCULANEUM. The only indication of its existence are the ruins of a Norman church still visible on what is now a peninsula.

The LARGEST FARM in history was owned by Samuel McCaughey from Ballymena. It was in Australia's Northern Territory and was bigger than Northern Ireland.

At the ITALIA '90 World Cup, Ireland
reached the quarter-finals having scored
only two goals in five matches.

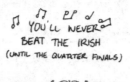

You'll never
beat the irish
(until the quarter finals)

ST. JOHN'S CATHEDRAL IN LIMERICK HAS THE TALLEST SPIRE IN IRELAND AT 94M.

The statue of QUEEN VICTORIA
outside the Queen Victoria Building in
Sydney, Australia once stood outside
Leinster House, Dublin.

HOW DID ONE
END UP IN THIS KIP?
WE ARE SERIOUSLY
NOT AMUSED.

The person who 'blew his mind out in a car' in the famous Beatles song 'A DAY IN THE LIFE', was Tara Brown, an heir to a Guinness fortune. He is buried in a grave on the shores of Luggula Lake in Co. Wicklow.

IN IRELAND THE LIFE EXPECTANCY FOR A MAN IS 75.44 YEARS.

Toaiseach Jack Lynch, discussing the ban on condoms, once said that he'd decided to 'put the issue on the LONG FINGER'.

The name 'CURRAGH' literally means 'racecourse'. The first recorded race took place at the Curragh in 1727 although it's thought races have been held there for 2000 years.

Leopardstown in Dublin derives its name
from the Irish, *Baile an Lobhair*, meaning
'TOWN OF THE LEPERS'.

**LAYTOWN RACES IN MEATH IS THE
ONLY OFFICIAL IRISH RACE MEETING
RUN ON A BEACH.**

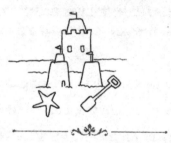

Shane McGowan of The Pogues first played
with a 1977 English punk band called
'THE NIPPLE ERECTORS'.

**DESPITE BEING LESS THAN
100KM FROM WALES, WHICH HAS
ONE OF THE WORLD'S RICHEST COAL
FIELDS, IRELAND IS VIRTUALLY
DEVOID OF COAL.**

The RED HAND on the Ulster flag comes from a legend about a boat race between rival chieftains, the winner being awarded the kingship of Ulster. The victor would be the one whose hand first touched the shore. Losing as he approached the land, the chieftain Heremon O'Neill so loved Ulster that he cut off his hand and threw the bloodied appendage ashore, so claiming victory.

EW! TAKE IT IF YOU WANT IT THAT BAD!

Officially, a FREEMAN OR FREEWOMAN of Dublin must own a bow, a coat of mail, a helmet and a sword.

SOCRATES, one of the greatest
Brazilian soccer players of the 70s/80s,
once played for UCD football club.

**MOLES, COMMON IN BRITAIN,
ARE ABSENT FROM IRELAND.**

The interior of the largest church
in Ireland, ST PATRICK'S CATHEDRAL,
Dublin, could fit sideways into St Peter's in
Rome with 70 metres to spare.

PADRAIG HARRINGTON is the only southern Irishman ever to win a golfing major. And he's won three. Fred Daly from Northern Ireland won one in 1947.

AT THE 1908 OLYMPICS, IRISH ATHLETES COMPETING FOR OTHER COUNTRIES WON 23 MEDALS, INCLUDING 8 GOLDS.

OFFALY is the only county to have won a GAA All Star in every position in both hurling and football.

DRACULA written by Dubliner Bram Stoker in 1897, has never once been out of print.

The LONGEST DISTANCE you can travel in a straight line in Ireland is from a point on the north east coast of Antrim (to the east of Ballycastle) to a point on the south west coast of Cork, (to the east of Schull), a distance of 468km.

40% OF ALL SALES OF GUINNESS ARE IN AFRICA.

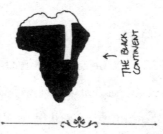

← THE BLACK CONTINENT

The Irish CROWN JEWELS were stolen in 1907 and the main suspect was Francis Shackleton, brother of the famed polar explorer, Ernest, although he was never charged.

U2 were originally called

'THE LARRY MULLEN BAND'

and used to practise in Larry's kitchen.

DIVORCE WAS LEGAL IN IRELAND UNTIL 1937.

Muckross Lake, near Killarney

in Co. Kerry, is reputed to be the

DEEPEST LAKE in Ireland

at 64 metres.

The double-earpiece

STETHOSCOPE was invented by

Wexford doctor Arthur Leared.

Balbriggan was once famous worldwide for producing MEN'S LONG JOHNS, giving the male underwear the name 'Balbriggans', a term used several times by 19th century Wild West characters played by John Wayne.

HURLING HAS BEEN PLAYED IN IRELAND FOR AT LEAST 2000 YEARS.

Eurovision winner JOHNNY LOGAN played Gaelic football for the Louth minors.

♫ ♪ ♫ ♫♫♫ ♪
HOLD ME NOW

TWO COUNTRIES BECAME REPUBLICS IN 1949, IRELAND AND CHINA.

The national symbol of Ireland is not
the shamrock, but the Celtic harp.

MOUNTJOY SQUARE is
supposedly the only square in Dublin
that is actually square.

**DANNY LA RUE, THE FAMOUS
DRAG ARTIST, WAS BORN DANIEL
PATRICK CARROLL IN CORK CITY.**

In 1895, MICHAEL CLEARY from
Clonmel was tried for the murder of his
wife Bridget, who he had burned to death
because he believed she had been replaced
by a fairy changeling. He was found
guilty of manslaughter.

James Cameron was unhappy with the
performance of Gaelic Storm, the Irish
band who appear in the film TITANIC,
when they first played on set. They
explained that when he'd seen them play
live they'd been pissed. Cameron
immediately ordered more beer to be
brought on set until the band were sozzled
enough to perform to the director's liking.

— KEEP DRINKING LADS!

Although NEWGRANGE is over
5000 years old, some of the markings
inside were later discovered to be graffiti,
probably made by plundering Vikings
around AD750.

The term 'NOSEY PARKER' originated with a British soldier, Edward Parker, stationed in Laois, who had an unfortunate tumour on his protuberance so that his nose almost reached his chin.

In ancient Irish Brehon Law there were seven forms of MARRIAGE. The seventh form, a seventh degree union, was a one-night stand.

WHERE IS OUR LOVE GOING TO TAKE US?

ALL THE WAY TO A 7TH DEGREE UNION.

SWORDS in north County Dublin, a small village in the 1960s, is now the eighth largest town in the Republic of Ireland.

The two mountains on the Cork-Kerry border, called 'THE PAPS', were believed to be the breasts of the ancient fertility goddess Anu. Each of the Paps has a large nipple-like cairn on its summit.

Field Marshall HORATIO KITCHENER, famous as the face of the WWI recruitment posters bearing the pointing finger and the slogan, 'Your Country Needs You', was from Kerry.

Lough Corrib in Galway has an ISLAND for every day of the year – 365 in total.

The first ever colour picture on the
front of *The Irish Times* showed
STEPHEN ROCHE on the Tour de France
winner's podium in 1987.

'IT'S A LONG WAY TO TIPPERARY'
WAS WRITTEN BY TWO ENGLISHMEN,
JACK JUDGE AND HARRY WILLIAMS.

The internationally regarded OPERA, The
Bohemian Girl, was composed by Dubliner
William Balfe.

PATRICK IS THE 42ND MOST
POPULAR FIRST NAME IN THE US.

The 8,630 foot high MOUNT CREAN
in Antarctica is named after Kerryman and
polar explorer, Tom Crean.

DRINKING CHOCOLATE

was invented in the late 1600s by Sir
Hans Sloane from County Down who
was President of the Royal College
of Physicians.

KEVIN MORAN is the only person
ever to win a GAA All Ireland Football Final
medal and an FA Cup Final Medal.

It took 114 English FA Cup Finals before
a player was finally sent off – **KEVIN
MORAN** of Manchester United in 1985.

During Ireland's ICE AGE (which
ended 10,000 years ago) every piece of
land above a line from north Kerry to
Waterford was completely
covered in ice.

**IN 1914, THE GUINNESS BREWERY
AT ST JAMES'S GATE, DUBLIN, WAS
THE LARGEST BREWERY IN THE
WORLD.**

The Liffey was once so polluted
with sewage that writer and playwright
BRENDAN BEHAN described the annual
Liffey Swim as 'Going through the motions'.

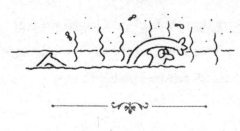

FASTNET ROCK is not the most
southerly point of Ireland. This title belongs
to Little Fastnet, a much smaller rock
30 metres to the south.

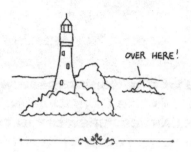

OVER HERE!

The Transport Workers' Union
of America was founded by a Kerry
republican activist, MIKE QUILL,
in 1934.

The LAST WOMAN HANGED in
Ireland was Annie Walsh, aged 31, who
was executed in 1925 for having murdered
her husband with an axe.

The world's most popular SHORTHAND system, Gregg Shorthand, was invented by Irishman John Robert Gregg from Co. Monaghan.

THE BORDER BETWEEN THE REPUBLIC AND NORTHERN IRELAND IS 360 KILOMETRES LONG.

Irish-American JOHN F KENNEDY is the only Catholic ever to be elected President of the US.

THE DRIEST YEAR ON RECORD IN IRELAND WAS 1887.

Renowned County Clare writer, EDNA O'BRIEN'S first three books were banned because of their sexual content.

BAILEYS IRISH CREAM, launched in 1974, was the first cream liqueur in the world.

There are three UNESCO world heritage sites on the island of Ireland, Brú na Bóinne, Skellig Michael and the Giant's Causeway. The Rock of Cashel is under consideration.

MAYBE IF IT HAD A ROOF?

When the VIKINGS firmly established themselves in Waterford in AD914, it became Ireland's first city.

The first successful FLIGHT ACROSS
THE ATLANTIC from east to west was
completed on April 13, 1928 by Irishman
James Fitzmaurice, taking off from
Baldonnel Aerodrome, Dublin and landing
on Greenly Island, Quebec, Canada.

**1,390 SQ KM OF IRELAND'S TOTAL
AREA IS UNDER WATER.**

When the British were handing
over power to MICHAEL COLLINS in
1922, Lord Lieutenant FitzAlan remarked
that Collins had arrived seven minutes late
for the ceremony. Collins replied, 'We've
been waiting over seven hundred years, you
can have the extra seven minutes.'

The term 'YAHOO',
nowadays meaning a yobbo or hooligan,
was coined by Irish writer Jonathan Swift
as the name of the race of sub-humans or
de-evolved humans in *Gulliver's Travels*.

**3 IRISH COUNTIES HAVE
NO CINEMA – CAVAN, LAOIS
AND ROSCOMMON.**

IRISH COFFEE was invented
by Joseph Sheridan, the head chef at
Shannon International Airport
in the 1940s.

HARRY GEORGE FERGUSON, one of
the founders of the international tractor
company Massey Ferguson, made the first
powered flight in Ireland, travelling 118.5 m
in a monoplane he had built himself.

**IN 2006, THE US RETAIL
FEDERATION REPORTED THAT 93
MILLION AMERICANS PLANNED TO
WEAR GREEN ON ST PATRICK'S DAY.**

GEORGE BARRINGTON was Ireland
and Britain's most infamous pickpocket in
the early 19th century. He once picked a
snuff box from Russian Count Orlov worth
£30,000 (millions by today's standards).

Thomas John Barnardo, the founder of the famous children's charity, BARNARDO'S, was from Dublin.

In 2004 Ireland became the first country in the world to introduce a comprehensive SMOKING BAN in all workplaces.

As of 2009, Ireland's top ten RICHEST people have over €8 billion between them.

The most popular Irish SURNAME in the US is Moore, in ninth place.

SHELTA IS A LANGUAGE SPOKEN BY MANY OF THE IRISH TRAVELLER COMMUNITY.

RONAN KEATING is in the *Guinness Book of Records* for being the only artist ever to have 30 consecutive top ten singles in the UK chart, out-scoring even the Beatles and Elvis.

YOU COULD FIT IRELAND INTO THE USA 130 TIMES.

At its peak in 1920, Ireland had 5,500 kilometres of RAILWAY LINE.

Irish nationalist CONSTANCE MARKIEWICZ was the first woman to be elected to the British House of Commons.

15,000 YEARS AGO YOU COULD HAVE WALKED FROM IRELAND TO SCOTLAND OVER A LAND BRIDGE.

Navan-born PIERCE BROSNAN'S first movie role was in the 1980 London gangster film, 'The Long Good Friday', in which he appeared in just a handful of brief scenes playing the role of '1st Irishman'.

In 1871, the murderer of bank
official William Glass in Newtownstewart,
Tyrone, turned out to be T H Montgomery,
the DETECTIVE who was
investigating the case.

**JAMESON IS THE BIGGEST SELLING
IRISH WHISKEY IN THE WORLD.**

The first IMMIGRANT to officially enter
the United States through the Ellis Island
facility in New York was a young Irish girl
called Annie Moore. A statue of her marks
both her departure point in Cobh, County
Cork and at Ellis Island.

**DANIEL O'CONNELL WAS ONCE THE
LORD MAYOR OF DUBLIN.**

The largest STONE CIRCLE in Ireland is at Lough Gur in County Limerick. It is 50 metres in diameter and has 113 standing stones, the largest of which is 4 metres high and weighs 40 tons. It was built 4000 years ago.

LEGENDARY BELFAST FOOTBALLER, GEORGE BEST PLAYED FOR 9 DIFFERENT FOOTBALL CLUBS, INCLUDING CORK CELTIC.

PATRICIA is the second most popular female given name in the US. Mary is first.

Fastnet Island used to be known as
'IRELAND'S TEARDROP' as it was
often the last piece of their homeland that
emigrants would ever see.

The British built
50 MARTELLO TOWERS around
Ireland to watch for an invasion by
Napoleon that never came.

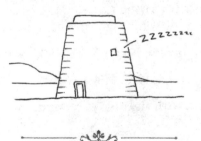

A large percentage of ICELAND'S
population are the descendants of Irish
slaves brought there by Norsemen in the
ninth century.

ALCOCK AND BROWN made the first
non-stop transatlantic flight in June 1919,
crash-landing in a bog near Clifden,
Co. Galway which, from the sky, looked like
a level green field. Both airmen survived.

THANK YOU FOR
FLYING ALCOCK & BROWN.
WE HOPE YOU HAD
A PLEASANT FLIGHT...

Famous director Stanley Kubrick's highly
regarded movie, BARRY LYNDON, was shot
mostly around Powerscourt House,
Wicklow, with the area playing itself, England
and Prussia.

POWERSCOURT WATERFALL in Wicklow
is Ireland's highest waterfall at
121 metres or 400 feet.

Kilkenny hurling team are known
as THE CATS from the phrase 'to fight
like a Kilkenny cat', originating from
stories of how people used to make cats
fight each other to the death, often
with their tails tied together.

**THE LUSITANIA, REGARDED
AS THE SECOND MOST FAMOUS
MARITIME DISASTER AFTER THE
TITANIC, WAS SUNK BY A GERMAN
U-BOAT JUST OFF THE OLD HEAD
OF KINSALE, COUNTY CORK ON
7 MAY 1915 WITH THE LOSS
OF 1,198 LIVES.**

Two DOGS, the property of first
class passenger, survived the sinking
of the Titanic.

John Jesus Flanagan from Limerick,
competing for the USA, won the
OLYMPIC HAMMER-THROWING
gold medal at the 1900, 1904 and 1908
Olympic Games.

AH JESUS JOHN
WILL YE WATCH
WHERE YOU THROW
THAT BLEEDIN'
THING!

ENYA'S REAL NAME IS EITHNE PATRICIA NÍ BHRAONÁIN.

BONO reputedly got his name from
a hearing aid shop in North Earl Street,
Dublin called 'Bonavox', which literally
translates as 'good voice'. He subsequently
shortened it to Bono.

The town of BUTTEVANT in Cork is believed to derive its name from the war cry of the Barry family, 'Boutez-en-Avant' meaning 'strike forward'.

The Marxist revolutionary Che Guevara's full name was CHE GUEVARA LYNCH, as both his parents were of Irish-Spanish descent.

Hollywood actor MEL GIBSON'S first name comes from Saint Mel, a fifth-century Irish saint, while his second name, Colm-Cille, comes from a sixth-century Irish saint.

THE PERIMETER OF THE PHOENIX PARK IS 11 KILOMETRES LONG.

The world's first CHEESE & ONION flavoured crisp was invented in 1954 by Joe 'Spud' Murphy, founder of Tayto Crisps.

James Martin from Co. Down invented the world's first EJECTOR SEAT in 1945. The following year the first live test subject, Bernard Lynch, was launched into the air and landed safely.

Up to the early 1980s, a towering chimney stood on Shelbourne Road, Ballsbridge, Dublin across which was emblazoned a HUGE SWASTIKA. The chimney was part of The Swastika Laundry, which had operated there up to the late 1960s. The odd-looking landmark has since been demolished.

The name TALLAGHT is derived from '*támh leacht*', meaning 'plague burial place'.

Although GREEN is the colour most associated with Ireland, St Patrick's cloak was actually blue and St Patrick's Blue is the official colour of the Presidential Standard and on the coat of arms of Ireland.

60,000 BABIES ARE BORN IN IRELAND EVERY YEAR.

In 1916, Irish polar explorer ERNEST SHACKLETON travelled 800 miles in a small whale boat across towering polar seas to South Georgia Island to get help for his stranded crew. Shackleton and two of the men then crossed the mountains of South Georgia with just 50 feet of rope for climbing to reach a whaling station. All his crew were eventually rescued.

The name IRELAND comes
from the Celtic mother goddess Ériu,
giving us Eire.

**MURPHY IS THE MOST
COMMON NAME IN IRELAND.**

Irish-born TV personality
GRAHAM NORTON'S real name is
Graham William Walker.

**THE LEASE ON ST JAMES'S GATE
BREWERY DOESN'T EXPIRE UNTIL
THE YEAR 10759.**

← THIS IS A REALLY IMPORTANT BIT OF TRIVIA

Here's an interesting piece of trivia: the word trivia comes from the Latin words *tri* and *via*, meaning three roads. This was where people met, stopped for a chat and exchanged useless bits of oul' blather. In their lifetime, Colin Murphy and Donal O'Dea have spent so much time exchanging such useless bits of oul' blather about Ireland (mostly in pubs), that they are considered genuine Irish trivia experts, mostly by themselves. Mr Murphy and Mr O'Dea have enjoyed several successful collaborations in the past, usually involving avoiding paying for their rounds, but also through the hugely popular *Feckin' Books* series, now proudly reaching its 13th title. Mr Murphy, who is married to Grainne and has a couple of temperamental and expensive teenagers, used to work (loose definition) in the advertising industry but now works as a writer full time. Mr O'Dea is also married, to Karen, and they have three urchins to feed. He is currently employed as the Creative Director of a leading Irish advertising agency and has several bad habits of his own to feed as well.

Bibliography

Byrne, Alan, *Thin Lizzy: Soldiers of Fortune*. Canada: Firefly Publishing, 2005
Hitler, Bridget, Ed. Michael Unger, *The Memoirs of Bridget Hitler*. London:
  Duckworth, 1979
Llywelyn, Morgan, *A Pocket History of Irish Rebels*. Dublin: The O'Brien Press, 2000
MacDermott, Eithne, *Clann Na Poblachta*. Cork: Cork University Press, 1998
MacGregor, George, *The History of Burke and Hare and of the Resurrectionist Times,
  a fragment from the criminal annals of Scotland*. T D Morison, 1884
O'Farrell, Mick, *50 Things You Didn't Know About 1916*. Cork: Mercier Press, 2009
O'Farrell, Padraic, *The Mercier book of Irish Records*. Cork: Mercier Press, 1978
1916 Rebellion Handbook. Dublin: Mourne River Press, 1998
Rodgers, Thomas, *Irish-American Units in the Civil War*. Oxford: Osprey, 2008
Wallace, Martin, *A little History of Ireland*. Belfast: Appletree Press, 1998
2008 Guinness Book of Records
National Retail Federation of America - St. Patrick's Day.
Teagasc - The Irish Agriculture and Food Development Authority
US Census Bureau

NEWSPAPERS AND MAGAZINES
Hot Press Archive – Monto
Reville, William, *Ireland's Scientific Heritage*. The Irish Times, 2000
Slattery, Finbarr, *William Hill was one of the greatest of them all*. The Kingdom
Newspaper, 2003

WEBSITES
www.fai.ie
www.gaa.ie
www.britannica.com
http://www.met.ie
http://www.olympic.org/en
http://www.horslips.ie
http://www.sacred-texts.com - Dame Alice Kyteler
http://www.wikipedia.org
http://www.hotels.com - Top ten nudist beaches
http://www.lookaroundireland.com
http://www.reference.com

Get the whole Feckin' Collection ...

**FECKIN' BOOK OF IRISH SAYINGS
● IRISH SLANG ● IRISH QUOTATIONS ● IRISH
SONGS ● 2ND BOOK OF IRISH SLANG
● IRISH RECIPES ● IRISH SEX & LOVE
● IRISH INSULTS ● BANKERS & BOWSIES**

**ALSO AVAILABLE:
WHAT ARE WE FECKIN' LIKE? ●
THE FECKIN' BOOK OF EVERYTHING IRISH
● THE FECKIN' BOOK OF IRISH HISTORY ● THE
FECKIN' BOOK OF IRISH LOVE AND NOW
THAT'S WHAT I CALL A BIG FECKIN'
IRISH BOOK**

www.obrien.ie